BACK FROM NEAR EXTINCTION

AMERICAN BISON

by Anita Yasuda

Content Consultant
Jennifer Barfield, PhD
Special Assistant Professor, Animal Reproduction
Colorado State University

Core Library
An Imprint of Abdo Publishing
abdopublishing.com

abdopublishing.com

Published by Abdo Publishing, a division of ABDO, PO Box 398166, Minneapolis, Minnesota 55439. Copyright © 2017 by Abdo Consulting Group, Inc. International copyrights reserved in all countries. No part of this book may be reproduced in any form without written permission from the publisher. Core Library™ is a trademark and logo of Abdo Publishing.

Printed in the United States of America, North Mankato, Minnesota
072016
012017

THIS BOOK CONTAINS
RECYCLED MATERIALS

Cover Photo: David Hosking/Science Source
Interior Photos: David Hosking/Science Source, 1; Shutterstock Images, 4, 43; North Wind Picture Archives, 7; Ricardo Reitmeyer/iStockphoto, 9; iStockphoto, 12, 27; Red Line Editorial, 15, 38; B. G. Smith/Shutterstock Images, 17; Charles Schug/iStockphoto, 18, 45; MPI/Getty Images, 20, 23; Tony Campbell/Shutterstock Images, 25; Michael Weber/ImageBROKER RM/Glow Images, 28; Betsy Blaney/AP Images, 30; Science Source, 34; Matthew Brown/AP Images, 36; John Doman/The St. Paul Pioneer Press/AP Images, 39

Editor: Marie Pearson
Series Designer: Jake Nordby

Publisher's Cataloging-in-Publication Data

Names: Yasuda, Anita, author.
Title: American bison / by Anita Yasuda.
Description: Minneapolis, MN : Abdo Publishing, 2017. | Series: Back from near
    extinction | Includes bibliographical references and index.
Identifiers: LCCN 2016945422 | ISBN 9781680784633 (lib. bdg.) |
    ISBN 9781680798487 (ebook)
Subjects: LCSH: American bison--Juvenile literature.
Classification: DDC 599.64--dc23
LC record available at http://lccn.loc.gov/2016945422

CONTENTS

CHAPTER ONE

MAKING A COMEBACK

Rays of sun creep over the horizon. The morning calm is broken. A distant rumble grows louder and louder. It is not a storm but the noise of hooves. A small herd of bison is waking up. Like a slow freight train, they cross the meadow. The herd slows. Now that it is summer, they no longer have to push the snow from the sod. They take short steps while eating mouthfuls of grass and

Bison shed their thick winter fur when the weather gets warmer.

A Big Influence

Bison had a large effect on their habitat. They were the largest herbivore on the plains. When they were removed from the plains, many other plants and animals also disappeared. Now groups are working to save the plains. The bison are an important part of this work. Bison droppings contain plant seeds. Their hooves mix the soil and bury these seeds. In 2005 bison were brought back to Grasslands National Park. It is on the Montana and Saskatchewan border. Bison have changed the habitat in a good way. Many different native plants are once again growing in areas where there were few before.

plants. The sun beats down on their shaggy brown capes of fur. When the herd has taken its fill, it is time to rest. Most of the bison lie in the grass. They make deep sighs as they fold their legs beneath their large bodies. But two bulls are restless. They lower their heads and snort. Their fury grows. Who is strongest? They paw the ground and charge. Their large horns hook as they battle head-to-head.

Threats to Bison

Once, grasslands covered one-third of North

Native Americans used bison hide to make clothing items such as gloves.

America. These lands were home to more than 30 million bison. They were a source of food and materials for native peoples. In the 1800s, the sound of bison faded. Settlers and sport hunters began killing bison faster than bison could be born. Bison lost their habitat to farming, towns, and railroads. By the late 1800s, there were only 1,091 bison left.

GPS

A few parks use global positioning system (GPS) radio collars to track their bison. GPS uses satellite technology to provide precise location information. It tells researchers the bison's food preferences. Vets at Prince Albert National Park in Canada make sure that their bison are safe while collars are attached to them. First, they work with a helicopter pilot to locate the bison. The vet darts the bison with a special gun. The dart holds drugs that make the bison fall sleep. While the bison is asleep, the vet checks its health. The bison is fitted with a GPS collar. The collar lasts approximately two years until the battery dies.

Some people saw that bison were in danger, and they took action. Ranchers caught bison and raised them on their land. Later, governments in the United States and Canada set aside land to protect them.

Over time, bison herds grew. But there are still reasons to be concerned about the bison. As of 2016, 500,000 bison belonged to privately owned herds. However, these bison are not raised to conserve the species. They are raised for their meat and hides.

Bison once roamed the Great Plains. Today their range is restricted to parks and reserves.

There are only approximately 4,000 bison in public herds. Some ranchers believe that these public herds carry disease. They fear that bison could make their cattle ill. But most scientists believe that there is no threat from wild bison to cattle. Still, most public herds are kept behind fences. Bison cannot maintain the grassland ecosystem while fenced in. Scientists fear that, in time, bison behavior may change. Wild bison held behind fences may begin to act more like livestock.

Grasslands

Habitat loss is another threat to the bison. Once, bison called land from Canada to northern Mexico home. Now bison live on less than 1 percent of their original range. They are found in a few parks, ranches, and zoos across North America. But without more land, bison herds will not be able to grow. A lack of land also makes it harder to find new places for bison to live.

As of 2016, the population of bison herds is stable. But bison are listed as a near-threatened species. Bison depend on people to keep them safe and protect their habitat. If these efforts stopped, scientists believe the bison could face a greater risk. Bison could become endangered again. This is why bison still need the help of conservation groups today.

Dale F. Lott was a professor who studied the bison for many years. In his book *American Bison: A Natural History*, he wrote about bison biology and conservation:

> *The buffalo's hairbreadth escape from extinction was a conservation triumph. . . . But we still haven't done very well by them. Most of them . . . live in populations so small that they will suffer gene loss. If we are going to keep wild bison wild, we're going to have to protect the spaces they have, and we should look for some more space—space on the grasslands that shaped them and that they shaped in turn. A grassland park, or parks, would help a lot. And we should consider solving this paradox: [The bison] is the only wild animal in the United States that is not allowed to live as a wild animal—live outside parks and refuges—anywhere in its original range.*
>
> Source: Dale F. Lott. American Bison: A Natural History. Berkeley, CA: University of California Press, 2009. Print. 201.

Back It Up

Lott is using evidence to support a point. Write a paragraph describing the point the author is making. Then write down two or three pieces of evidence the author uses to make the point.

CHAPTER TWO

ALL ABOUT THE BISON

Bison belong to a group of mammals called ungulates. These animals have hooves. Many ungulates, including the bison, can run fast. Bison can run at up to 35 miles per hour (55 km/h). There are two types of American bison. They are the wood bison and the plains bison. The main difference between the two animals is size. Male wood bison stand up to 6 feet (2 m) tall at their hump. They

Bison hooves churn the soil. This helps plants grow.

Sense of Smell

A bison's nose is shaped like a triangle. It is flat, wide, and highly sensitive. It uses its nose to tell other animals apart from up to 1.9 miles (3 km) away. A bison makes this sense sharper by licking its nose. When a scent molecule touches the moist nose, the scent sticks to it. This makes the scent stronger. A good sense of smell makes it harder for a predator to sneak up on a bison.

can weigh more than 2,000 pounds (900 kg). Plains bison are often smaller and lighter than wood bison. Females of both species are smaller and weigh less than males. Males and females of both species have short black horns.

Due to their size, few predators attack bison. But bears and wolves have been known to. They usually prey on calves or on bison that are sick or old. The bison's large build helps them move deep snow with their heads. They swing their heads from side to side to dig to the grass below. All bison are born with rust-red fur. Their fur darkens with age to brown. Wood bison have wooly hair on their bodies. But

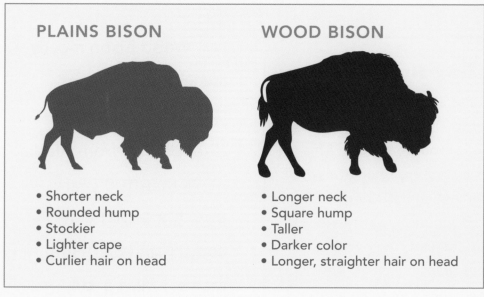

PLAINS BISON

- Shorter neck
- Rounded hump
- Stockier
- Lighter cape
- Curlier hair on head

WOOD BISON

- Longer neck
- Square hump
- Taller
- Darker color
- Longer, straighter hair on head

Which Is Which?
These diagrams show a wood bison and a plains bison. Notice their physical differences. How do you think the differences help them in their different habitats?

plains bison have short hair, which makes them better suited to hot summers on the plains. Hunters once killed bison for these hides. In 1872 one hide sold for $2 or $3, approximately $39 or $59 today.

Habitat

Bison graze throughout the day. They need to live in areas with lots of grass and other green plants. But today they suffer from range loss caused by people. Smaller ranges make it harder to find enough food.

All-Day Buffet

Bison eat all day long. They eat approximately 24 pounds (11 kg) of food each day. This works out to approximately 1.6 percent of their body mass. Bison never stand while eating. Instead, they walk and eat grasses, herbs, and twigs as they move. Bison swallow their food and then bring it back up. They chew on it again before finally digesting it.

Wood bison mostly live in northwestern Canada. They had disappeared from Alaska more than 100 years ago. But in 2015, 100 wood bison were brought back to Alaska. Wood bison graze in low, wet areas around lakes and rivers. In the summer, they eat plants such as willow leaves.

Plains bison live farther south. They graze on land with plenty of short and long grass. Bison usually need to drink water daily. Their range needs streams, rivers, or watering holes. When water is hard to find, bison can go a few days without it. During the winter, they might eat snow if they cannot find water.

There are approximately 11,000 wood bison in conservation herds. Many live in Canada.

Bison wallow for many reasons. One is to help shed their fur.

Life in the Herd

For most of the year, bison live in small groups. Each group has approximately 10 to 20 bison. Adult males usually do not live with females unless it is mating season. The mating season, called the rut, begins in late July and lasts until fall. During the rut, bulls make loud grunts to impress female bison in order to mate. The grunts can be heard miles away. Females give birth to a single calf in the spring. Bison calves can usually walk within an hour of birth.

In the summer, bison paw and roll on the ground. This behavior is called wallowing. It helps them scratch itchy insect bites. It also rids them of unwanted hair. So many bison may roll in the same spot that the ground begins to look like a dish. It is called a wallow. When bison wallow, they stir seeds into the soil. More plants grow, which in turn attracts other animals.

EXPLORE ONLINE

Chapter Two focused on the characteristics of bison and their habitat. It also touched on life in a bison herd. The website below gives more information about bison behavior. As you know, every source is different. How is the information given in the website different from the information in this chapter? What information is the same? How do the two sources present information differently? What can you learn from this website?

Animal Facts: Bison
mycorelibrary.com/american-bison

CHAPTER THREE

THREATS TO BISON

People have been the biggest danger to the bison's survival. Two hundred years ago, there were more than 30 million bison in North America. People traveling west wrote of seeing huge herds. Travelers said that bison filled the land as far as one could see. By the late 1800s, there were only a few hundred left.

Large herds of bison roamed North America in the early 1800s.

What Happened to the Bison?

In the 1800s, farmers and ranchers came west. They wanted to farm and raise cattle on the grasslands. As farmers planted crops, they destroyed grass, the bison's main source of food. Ranchers killed bison to make way for their animals. As more people came, bison were forced to live in smaller and smaller areas.

Bison moved farther west, but so did settlers. Railroad companies put down tracks in areas that bison had always grazed. The tracks brought trains full of hunters. Hunters shot as many bison as they could. The plains tribes of Native Americans

Bison Ties to Plains Tribes

The bison was the most important animal to tribes on the plains. For centuries, Native Americans lived alongside the bison. They used every part of the animal. They made rope, thread, teepee coverings, and clothing from bison. They created myths and legends around the bison. By the 1700s, some tribes used horses to hunt herds of bison. They traded extra hides to Europeans for guns and other goods.

Hunters killed millions of bison during the 1800s.

that already lived in the West used every part of a bison. They made clothes, teepees, jewelry, spoons, and many other things from a bison. But sport hunters left bison to rot on the plains by the thousands. As the number of bison dropped, demand for their bones grew.

Settlers began picking through the long grass for these bones. On average, bison bones sold for $8 a ton, approximately $145 today. It took approximately 100 bison skeletons to make 1 ton (0.9 metric tons) of bones. Some pickers found up to 50 tons (45 metric tons) of bones in a single spot. Trains took the bones to factories in the East. They were ground up for fertilizer or bone china. When the slaughter ended, the bison were nearly all gone. It also meant the end of a way of life for Native American tribes on the plains. These tribes had built their lives and culture around the bison.

Disease

As settlers and their animals moved closer to bison, they spread diseases. A lung disease called tuberculosis made it difficult for bison to breathe. Predators ate these weak animals. A more serious disease was brucellosis. This disease can cause calves to be stillborn. Fewer calves makes it harder for the bison population to grow. Today, there are wild wood

Brucellosis can cause bison cows to produce less milk for their young.

Not Welcome

In the summer, bison in Yellowstone National Park graze at higher elevations. In the winter, they move to lower, milder areas. For years, bison were not welcome outside the park. Ranchers feared that bison's diseases might spread to their cattle. In 2015 Montana's governor finally agreed to allow bison outside Yellowstone. It was the first time in 100 years that bison could roam parts of the state all year long.

bison herds in northern Canada that have both diseases. But many other plains and wood bison herds in the country are disease free.

In the United States, wood bison populations are disease free. Most herds of plains bison are also healthy. Only a few bison in the Yellowstone herd carry brucellosis. Because of this, ranchers want bison kept off lands outside the park. But there are no cases of cattle becoming ill from these bison. Elk in the area also have the disease. But they are not kept behind fences. Today, science is helping people better understand how the disease spreads. There is still no treatment.

Brucellosis can also infect elk.

Bison with small amounts of cattle DNA can look a lot like pure bison.

But researchers are hopeful that someday they will better understand how to deal with it.

DNA

Bison are also at risk from cattle genes. In the late 1800s, ranchers crossed cattle and bison. These hybrids are called cattalo. Those offspring with more cow DNA than bison DNA are also called beefalo. DNA is a type of code. It carries information about every part of a living thing. People thought that the new animals would be hardy like a bison and gentle like a cow. But they discovered that many of these cattaloes were not able to have young.

Most ranchers stopped trying to cross the two species. But some cattalo escaped and formed herds. As a result, more than 95 percent of bison have cattle DNA. Scientists also worry that the DNA within these herds is too alike. These herds were founded with only a few animals. When DNA is too alike, animals may have health problems. Now scientists are studying bison genes to keep future bison DNA diverse and healthy.

FURTHER EVIDENCE

There is much information about threats to bison in Chapter Three. What do you think is the main point of the chapter? What evidence was given to support that point? Visit the website below to learn more about threats to bison. Choose a quote from the website that relates to this chapter. Does this quote support the author's main point or make a new point? Write a few sentences explaining how the quote you found relates to this chapter.

The Buffalo War
mycorelibrary.com/american-bison

CHAPTER FOUR

BISON CONSERVATION

By the late 1800s, bison were on the verge of extinction. There were only approximately 325 wild bison left. Private citizens in Canada and the United States began to take steps to protect the bison. They feared that if nothing was done, bison would disappear.

Privately owned bison herds helped greatly increase wild bison populations.

Saving the Bison

The earliest attempts to protect the bison were made by cattle ranchers. Among them were Charles and Molly Goodnight. During the 1870s, the Goodnights caught four calves. They raised the calves with their cattle on their land. These calves were the beginning of a small bison herd. In time, bison from the Goodnight herd were sent all over the country, including to Yellowstone National Park.

Yellowstone already had a native herd of bison. In 1872 there were approximately 1,000 bison in the park. But many

Conservation across Borders

From the 1870s, ranchers Michel Pablo and Charles Allard raised bison. Their herd became one of the largest in the United States. When Allard died, Pablo tried to sell the herd to the US government. When this failed, he sold it to Canada for $245 a head. More than 300 plains bison were brought to Elk Island National Park in 1907. It became Canada's first wildlife sanctuary. In 2016, 89 bison from Elk Island were sent back home to the United States. The herd now lives on the Blackfeet Indian Reservation in Montana.

of these bison fell prey to poachers. In 1886 the US Army was put in charge of preventing poaching. But bison continued to be killed. There was no federal law that protected the bison. On May 7, 1894, Congress passed an act protecting all the birds and animals of Yellowstone National Park. Even still, the number of bison dropped to less than 50. Alarmed, Congress gave money to save the park's bison. Bison from private herds, including the Goodnight herd, were brought in to rebuild the wild herd.

National Bison Range

In 1905 conservationists formed the American Bison Society (ABS). They included President Theodore Roosevelt and natural scientist William Hornaday. They wanted to see small bison herds on reserves across the United States. The ABS successfully urged the US government to protect the bison. On May 23, 1908, the president signed the Bison Range Act. The act set aside $30,000 to buy land to protect the bison. The National Bison Range in Montana became one

William Hornaday was president of the ABS from 1907 to 1910.

of these areas. The ABS asked people to donate money to buy bison for this land. In the first year, the ABS collected more than $10,000. It used this money to buy bison from private herds. Today, the National Bison Range has between 325 and 350 bison. It is also home to many other types of wildlife, such as bighorn sheep and more than 200 types of birds.

Modern Conservation

Researchers today work to stop the spread of diseases that affect bison.

William Hornaday

In 1886 naturalist William Hornaday traveled to Montana. He was looking for a bison specimen for the United States National Museum at the Smithsonian Institution. The museum wanted it for an exhibit of North American mammals. Hornaday was shocked to find only a few bison left in areas where he had once seen many. He began educating people about conservation. In this role, Hornaday became the first director of the New York Zoological Park. In 1896 he was appointed director of the Bronx Zoo. In 1907 he established a bison herd at the zoo. You can still see bison at the Bronx Zoo today.

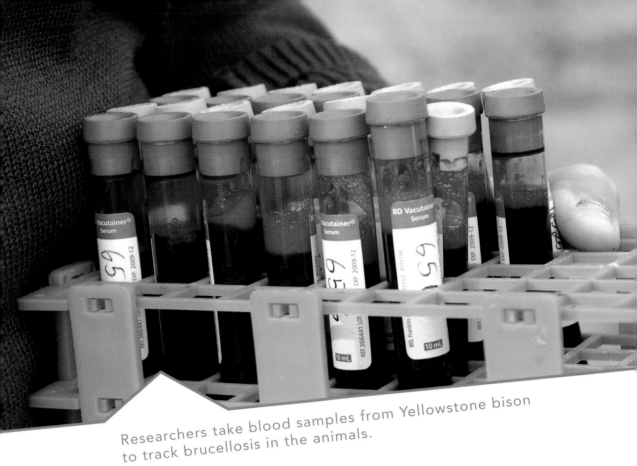

Researchers take blood samples from Yellowstone bison to track brucellosis in the animals.

Scientists at Colorado State University work with bison from Yellowstone's herd. The herd's genes are valuable. They contain no cattle DNA. The genes are also diverse. Originally, the bison came from several herds. But some of these animals carry brucellosis. Scientists have found a way to help save these animals using brand-new technology. First, they collect eggs and semen from Yellowstone's bison. These eggs and semen contain genes. Together, they make a bison embryo. The challenge begins in the lab. Here, scientists use chemicals to wash the embryos of disease. Scientists place the embryos in a disease-free bison cow. Nine months later, a healthy calf is born. Calves from this project now roam public lands in northern Colorado. One day calves such as these may help create bison herds all over the country. Scientists hope that techniques such as this will help the bison's comeback.

Scientists are also finding creative ways to save bison DNA. Many of today's herds now have cattle genes. At Texas A&M University, Dr. James Derr studies bison herds all over the country. Bison hair and blood are sent to Dr. Derr to test them for cattle genes. The testing can also tell which herd the animal is related to. People are using this information to create herds with a variety of genes. More diverse genes means that bison have a greater chance of surviving. These genetic tests are also being used

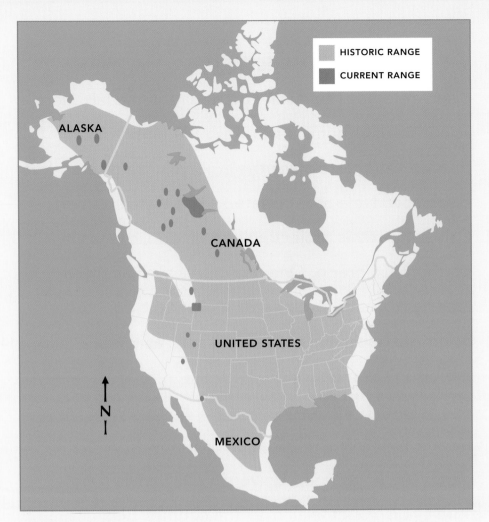

Bison Range

This map shows the historic and current range of the American bison. What do you notice about the change in the bison's range? How does this map help you understand the bison's plight today?

to start pure bison herds. One such herd is at Blue Mounds State Park in Minnesota. As of 2015, there were approximately 100 pure bison in the herd.

Blue Mounds' bison herd began in 1961.

Bison are no longer endangered. From the early
1900s, people became more aware of the danger
that bison were in. They took action to protect the
bison. They passed laws and set aside land to save

39

the species. These efforts helped the bison's numbers rise. But it is still important for people to care for bison. The bison population is still dependent on people. Bison need more land than they have been given to live on. As people work to conserve these lands, future bison herds will be even stronger.

The Yellowstone Association published a book explaining opportunities for and challenges of plains bison conservation at Yellowstone and across their historic range:

The lack of tolerance for wild bison in most areas outside Yellowstone National Park is the primary factor limiting their restoration in the Greater Yellowstone Area. . . . [T]here are political and social concerns about allowing bison outside the park, including human safety and property damage, competition with livestock and other ungulates for grass, diseases such as brucellosis that can be transmitted between bison and cattle, depredation of agricultural crops, and a shortage of funds for state management. . . . Fortunately, many of these constraints can be remedied through the collaborative actions of federal and state agencies across jurisdictional boundaries, and the future choices of people in Montana and elsewhere.

Source: Yellowstone Bison: Conserving an American Icon in Modern Society. *P. J. White, Rick L. Wallen, David E. Hallac, eds. Yellowstone National Park: Yellowstone Association, 2015. Print. 17.*

Point of View

Read both Straight to the Source texts in the book and think about the two points of view. How are they similar and why? How are they different and why?

Common Name

- Plains bison/wood bison

Scientific Name

- *Bison bison bison/Bison bison athabascae*

Average Size

- 5.5 to 6.1 feet (1.7–1.9 m) tall for adult males;
  5 to 5.1 feet (1.5–1.6 m) tall for adult females
- 1,199 to 2,000 pounds (544–907 kg) for adult males;
  701 to 1,202 pounds (318–545 kg) for adult females

Color

- Adult bison have dark brown to black hair; calves have reddish-brown hair

Diet

- Grass (bluestem, buffalo grass, and gama grass), weeds, lichens, flowering plants (sunflower), wood plant leaves (mesquite, elm)

Average Life Span

- 10 years in the wild; 20–35 years in captivity

Habitat

- Plains and grasslands of western North America, northern forests of Canada, and parts of southern Alaska

Threats

- Habitat loss, disease, cattle DNA, and low genetic diversity
- Endangered status: near threatened

STOP AND THINK

Tell the Tale

Chapter Three discusses how European settlers and sport hunters came into bison habitats. Imagine you belong to one of the plains tribes that depended on bison. Write 200 words about the settlers' and hunters' activities and how they affected the bison. Describe the changes that the Native American tribes experienced. What could people have done to protect the bison?

Surprise Me

Chapter Two discusses bison characteristics and behavior. After reading this book, what two or three facts about bison did you find most surprising? Write a few sentences about each fact. Why did you find them surprising?

Take a Stand

This book discusses how ranchers have limited the bison's range to make room for farms. Do you think farming is more important than the bison's range? Or do you think both are important? Why?

Another View

This book has much information about bison conservation. As you know, every source is different. Ask a librarian or another adult to help you find a reliable source about bison conservation. Write a short essay comparing the point of view of each author. How are they similar and why? How are they different and why?

GLOSSARY

conservation
preserving and protecting
something

digest
breaking down food into
nutrients the body can use

disease
a sickness

genes
parts of DNA that determine
appearance and other traits

GPS
the global positioning
system, which uses satellites
to find the locations of
objects

grassland
an open, grassy area of land
with few trees or shrubs

herbivore
an animal that survives by
eating plant material

poachers
people who illegally hunt wild
animals

predator
an animal that hunts and eats
other animals

range
an area where an animal lives

ungulates
animals with hooves

wallow
a dish-like area in which
animals roll or lie

LEARN MORE

Books

Erlic, Lily. *Grasslands*. New York: Weigl Publishers, 2006.

Patent, Dorothy Hinshaw. *The Buffalo and the Indians: A Shared Destiny*. New York: Clarion Books, 2006.

Tomljanovic, Tatiana. *Bison*. New York: AV2 by Weigl, 2011.

Websites

To learn more about Back from Near Extinction, visit **booklinks.abdopublishing.com**. These links are routinely monitored and updated to provide the most current information available.

Visit **mycorelibrary.com** for free additional tools for teachers and students.

INDEX

ABOUT THE AUTHOR

Anita Yasuda is the author of more than 100 books for children. She enjoys writing biographies, books about science and social studies, and chapter books. Anita lives with her family in Huntington Beach, California, where she often walks her dog along the shore.

BOOK CHARGING CARD

Accession No. _____ Call No. _____

Author _____

Title _____

Date Loaned	Borrower's Name	Date Returned